FINDING PEACHES

IN THE DESERT

FINDING PEACHES

IN THE DESERT

Pamela Uschuk

San Antonio, Texas
2000

Finding Peaches in the Desert © 2000 by Pamela Uschuk

First printing

ISBN: 0-930324-59-5

Wings Press
627 E. Guenther
San Antonio, Texas 78210
Ph/fax: (210) 271-7805

On-line catalogue and ordering:
www.wingspress.com

Cover painting,"Lady Boat Late Light,"
© 1991 by Bruce McGrew

CONTENTS

FINDING PEACHES IN THE DESERT

BATHING IN KACHINA HOT SPRINGS

CALENDAR OF THIRST

WAITING FOR RAIN

This book is dedicated with love to Bill and Jennifer,
dearest Roots of my matter,
and to my parents,
George (1917-1996) and Ella Uschuk

FINDING PEACHES

IN THE DESERT

We must learn to turn slaughter into food.

– Joy Harjo

FINDING PEACHES IN THE DESERT

They taste like a woman, you say
and bite deep into the sweet heat
squeezing through tender skin,
while I laugh, taking the fruit you offer.
We close our eyes and transport
this delicious host to our loves
flown distant as time in dreams.
You can never eat too many, I say and pull
another ripe peach from the desert tree.
It fills my palm, my mouth as I suck
the unhusbanded nectar.
It is delicious as stealing light,
such innocent grace, a holiday
from history and eternity.
We bare our breasts to sun
as women have done for centuries
beside the blue water pool at ease with rabbits, shrill
wasps, the shy steps of occasional deer,
while vultures funnel midheaven.
Struck dumb by sun cauterizing
the Sonoran sky that flings its blue skirt
all the way across the ripe hip of Mexico,
we feast on peach after peach, while
peach-colored tanagers, wet
green hummingbirds and the topaz eyes of lizards
attend our annointment.

When I wipe one quarter across my breasts
and down my stomach to my thighs, I
am amazed at the baked odor of love
rising from everything I touch.
This is our ceremony to alter the news
of troops that mass for attack
in the Middle East, to alchemize all hatred
and greed, whatever name
it is given by multinational interests.
There is no aggression in sharing rare fruit
priceless as the wide imaginings of sky
or the brilliant coinage of dragonfly wings.
Even squadrons of wasps and fire ants
armed with nuclear stingers turn
from attack to the pungency of this
ritual feast that celebrates love
in the desert stunned green by unusual rain.

THEORIES OF LIGHT

for Arnold Nelson

Old philosopher of stones and shade,
the striped lizard shakes fire ants free
from her delicate feet to jet,
                        slender hydrofoil, across the patio
where she rests at the corolla of sunlight
that blinds us like the half-formed idea of God
or the notion of immortality.

If chaos is the inventive mother
who crochets a neat doily, then
what is art or immortality to those who create?

Even as bodies evaporate
        to quarks pulsed back at distant galaxies,
what remains? Terrible beauty
that translates all languages, symmetry or
        dis of form and color
withstanding death's crazy weather. Or
just an idea to make us feel better?

Consider mortality as the fear of silence
even while the spirit swells like a Coltrane note
inside time's concentric riffs.

A good hunter knows to study the edges of his vision —
never look for the buck but for his movement.

So hungry we are for one ball bearing
        that caroms unchanged
through an eternal pinball machine of the imagination,
    we deny
the evidence of corpses, the sag of flesh from birth.

What's art worth?
No one's defined the center of a ghost
        that tattoos high desert noon—
black-barred glare liquid as neon,
irreducible,
      into which
even armored lizards and the mating cries of doves
    must disappear.

SCORPION SEASON

Heat and monsoons call them out.
Scorpions drop from ceilings
or hide inside the cool damp flesh of washcloths.
They find me everywhere
I don't want them to be.
Now, before coffee, I'm ready for a bath.
No alarm is more obscene
than this scorpion in my tub
who maps with translucent claws
the unscalable stainless drain.
Its caramel body glows, shows off
the one black vein of poison
that lashes the heart to the stinger tail.

Ticking seductress,
misfortune's naive face,
the scorpion scuttles through the world's shadows
with its tail held aloof,
lariat-looped above its delicate head.
Some call it beautiful
but I won't forget the night
a scorpion twice stung my breast.
Venom dry-iced my chest, constricted
my breath in its death vest.
My legs swelled numb and, for days,
pain's reggae needled my face, my hands.

Last night when the moon cracked thunderheads
and the arroyos yelped
from the hysterical hunting of coyotes,
I screamed when I found the scorpion
curled on my pillow.
Not this time, you
little son of a bitch!
I said as I clamped down the mayonnaise jar.

Then I heard it, the minute click
of his claws, their quick
and frantic tattoo on glass.
That small tapping rapped
from my own inner ear,
the fear of the blind man's stick,
electricity licking the fingernails of the dead.

I stopped, awed by the power
of so much venom in such a fragile shape.
Such charm the world offers
is as dangerous as the one lover
you'd follow anywhere.
The scorpion and I are not so different,
carrying poison to protect us,
plagued by our common baggage
of action and consequence.
I freed him, knowing such defenses are necessity
for those who live by thunderlight and moon.

This morning, I wonder if I made a mistake.
I am naked and shivering
despite the heat.

How do I evict this scorpion
from my bathtub without being stung?
Already, clouds knot blue air
and lightning spikes wind
through bloodskinned manzanita,
yellow-flowering mesquite
while I find the perfect instruments—
                              chopsticks!

Never has balance been more apparent.
This morning hovers between
punishment and grace.
Rain breaks as, in one
swift pinch and lift, I flip
the scorpion into its transparent cage.
Together we'll wait out the monsoon
in this dry land, where each day
we learn the heart of its seasons
are twins to ours
with their beauty, their terror.

SMOOTH RAZOR

Wasn't I once the party darling, lion-
haired blonde that flung gold arms
and thighs wild dancing,
yet so shy sometimes and scared
I couldn't tell the truth to anyone
but thickets of wild wrens and trilliums.
When the music stopped, wasn't I the big-eyed doe
who ran from men and boys,
      their terrible baby-laced sex
or the vamp who fell into some stoned bed, moaning
to the pounding surf in my temples,
riding deeper and deeper into suicidal light
the wet horse of need?

Now orange blossoms blow sweet nothings
across the lawn.   All the fawn-dappled clouds
paw desert mountains surrounding us,
and I remember how once I snorted into the shock of wind
riming Grand Traverse Bay at forty below,
while the thousand shattering panes of blue ice
piled skyscraper high against the shore,
and I prayed for love, *cherish is the word*
impossible love to save me, love's
chrome semi grill crashing into me,
a pure ratchet of light
cracking my young marriage-sledged brain, love
sharp and clean as gin,

an obsidian scalpel of love,
love's electrocuted smile,
any love from any lips anywhere.

      But nothing
showed up besides hangovers
and my husband's frigid hands,
his whiskeyed Irish breathing,
his catjumps away from embrace.   His constant casting
into cold runs for lunker trout to show the boys
he, too, was one of them, could
joke about tits, wine, his waders
peeled down to dry by his wife. His doomsday drum
snare-rattled the too late world, all hope
shot full of holes as any Belfast street.
Is it any wonder I leapt

      far into the charred arms of distances? Into
the buffalo dreams
of travel, crossing
and recrossing the continent
in a beatup green Impala, alone
except for my sweet mongrel, Ivan,
rug-sprawled across the backseat and demanding nothing
but the soft stroke and ruffle of love between his ears,
along his golden spine.

   Leapt into the anonymous rumples of lovers
who bolted, stung by the tail of love's wide syllable.
   Leapt finally into the black-haired arms
of the man my ex-husband warned was a smooth razor.

A razor was my desire
for this man hunkered like a grizzly,
his dark size topped by a mind precise as any Swiss hand
at work over the guts of a watch, mind
that could vault, soaring
like a Marsh Hawk surveying the tangle of swamp and field
updrafted with celestial light,
mind sweet as dark chocolate smeared
across a Mediterranean cheek, Corsican mind
blown in a sudden gust ridiculous
as a dragon kite turned inside out, spinning.

And didn't we spin? We were
two gale-force winds across the globe
bashing into one another, lifting
one another over oceans
and shores, onto the backs
of sweating horses
and their flat-out heart-burst gallop
through bee-buzzed sage.
Our laughter never aged. In movies
or over the comic page
we laughed against black fangs of doubt,
death's dumb fingers
that tried to strangle our verse.

Nearly two decades, we've leapt
into chocolate-covered orange rinds, raspberry pies
and midnight fights,
love bites and cross-country flights
to the biggest Apple
          and back. You always

come back
>to my lips, my hands, my thighs, tangling
your fingers in my hair.
>>>To the stink of roses
slicking the bedside lamp.

Now here I sit, eating a whole bag of potato chips
again, not caring to calculate what weight
they'll add to thigh and waist.
Wondering just how the far-flung future
caught up with me, I lick,
from my fingertips, salt, sweet
and lovely grease. Handsome healing blade,
we're in it for the long-term kiss.

CLEAN MEMORIALS

A Tarantula Hawk drags the limp Tarantula
twice its size across our prickly yard.
No Sisyphus, this wasp's resolute.
Its slender legs lift to negotiate mica, broken
feldspar, rotted cactus limbs and the dog
barking circles around it.
Streamlined as the orange fingernail of a courtesan
adorned with black lace wings, the wasp
is all business, an executive who never loses
a firm grasp on her stunned client.
Of course, our sympathy is with the spider
whose striped legs are soft and bump
vulnerable as anemone tentacles
against all thorns in sight,
those legs and the exposed fat furry belly
this wasp's larvae will suck dry.
Their meal will last weeks.
In the desert nothing is wasted—each corpse
is stripped to bone.
We must admire this strict attendance to the dead
that leaves such clean memorials to our lives.

FEEDING JAVELINAS IN THE FOOTHILLS

for Charlotte Lowe

Streamlined as tropical fish covered with a torrent
of the hair you'd find grizzled on wolves or badgers,
they show up at the sliding glass door
outside your kitchen.   Enormous, their heads
flow in one solid muscle to their shoulders
packed like boulders tapered
to the sine curve of their narrow hairy asses
as they snuffle across desert,
neat tuxedo hooves
ticking the concrete patio.
Their eyes sink like full inky moons
above tusks that could sever your arm.
When you offer small carrots
in your delicious fingers, javelinas
toss their wild snouts starward,
throats rumbling. It is a cross between
a washing machine scrubbing levis
and a howler monkey's leaflit love whoop.
So astonishing that sound and you bending,
a supplicant surrounded by the host
of these wild pigs, your neat blonde braid
like Challah braised in moonlight,
your eyes the blue of a cerulean warbler's wing
and your smile sweet and wicked above
scars that rivet your thigh.

Hold the carrot by the tip, you advise.
Their jaws are undercut so far
they could tear your fingers from the sure hold
of the knuckles.   Here.
And it is more than a dare or matter of trust
when I bend with you
to these beasts whose blank glares promise everything.
I hold out tender roots, entering
that wilderness and divining the gorgeous dark core
of fear with a friend who's been there before.

THE NIGHT MY FATHER BECAME
AN ABORIGINE

I

My father suffers the long trail of his dying
like my grandmother who passed everyone twelve years ago.
Cold as mountain snow, oxygen gusts
into his nose, oxygen the argument
urging his congestive heart to beat.

On the sage blown plateau where dreams cross memory,
he waits in his favorite chair welcoming the final shore.
Soldier he once roared against death's teeth,
now sees earth crack wide beside him,
the shovel engraved with his name.
He tells me he's ready, has no regrets while
regrets spurl like dustdevils deafening my ears.

How long have I clung to his life like
frail lace to an old ball gown?
Now thread unraveled, his advice
and stories drift disregarding time.

II

Tonight my husband and I attend
the Australian aboriginal performance
at Centennial Hall, where a small fire jigs

on the sand-coated stage, introducing us
to these public-secret dances.

Opening the audience, the diggerydo
halloos like the subaqueous murmur of whales
or the long moan of distant stars, while
a 60,000 year old man painted with white chalk and mud
clicks deft sticks in his leather hands,
amazing us with bellnotes he sings
deep as iron mined from earth,
his larynx strings replicating
the language of the bass viola
laying songlines from across the globe.

In 1942, these same aborigines
amazed my young father when,
drunk and AWOL from the Army Air Corps, he
hopped trains all the way around Australia, a final fling
before being shipped to New Guinea
where he would witness native Papuans
disemboweled and hung from trees by the Japanese
in a world war that would remodel his life.

My father cannot get over the enemy Japanese
nor his love of these aborigines
from his chair in the far livingroom of his dying.
A boomerang hangs above his woodstove, forever
slinging him back to Sydney, the great Barrier Reef
or the vast red Western Desert
where he crouched around campfires
sparking stars and trading stories with the fathers
of these men who entrance the stage.

When the chalked old man makes his final hop
into the circle of dancers, it is my father I see.
Relieved of his wheelchair,
the deafening bellow of the oxygen tank,
he is all electric leap, his bare feet
slapping the parquet floor,
his voice raised like a dingo's
ululating through the night.
It is such a beautiful song
I hum along, warmed by the distant fire
and stories where there is no real end
to the dreamtime or the dreamers.

ANOTHER FULL MOON POEM

This is the last insomniac poem I'll write.
I'm tired of Goddess Weepy Eye
wringing nostalgia into my brain's warm sink,
sick of the stinking worm skull that so loves
to gum the sponge of lonely hearts.

Like a semi's fast headlamp the full moon
smashes my rearview mirror
above the nattering of tires
on pavement cutting desert night.

It silvers the rattler oozing
through the last of the day's heat
shimmying asphalt berm.
Beluga white lunar light tongues
the granite nipples of the Rincon Mountains.

Moon, dented infant face, how many
love-thrummed hearts have you seized
like pistons frozen mid-thrust?
Lone stone with your bonecold eye
what is in your glance that frazzles, then
collapses the steaming trestles of dreams?

No longer will I stare into your stark caffeine
spiking midnight. What can I do
but love you as I love the tarantula

tippling from its half-eaten prey
to the mercury slurring your smile.

THE YEAR WE LIVED ABOVE
THE ALBINO DWARF

for Warren

Breaking our quarrels, your arias
ascended, feminine fingers soothing the bite
of metal bars dividing the cold air register,
those grace notes ruffling towels
black and white as lies about love and its lack.

Weeks after you moved to our basement,
your parents arrived to complain
my staccato boots banged hardwood floors
above your head. Why didn't you tell me
I shotgunned your coffee mugs to dance,
spazzed your fragile bone china wild?

When killdeer migrated under the midnight moon
and my love stayed late in bars, I paced
sock-footed, cried into goose down pillows
to hide grief that shook like the white birch
losing its tobacco-colored leaves.

Thinskinned, you and I jacked up the thermostat
watching snowdrifts finalize
the elegant spines of the Bitterroot Mountains.
Cutting fat from winter beef,
I muffled the knife's sharp slice

as my love and I wrote separate
versions of joy and misery
into the season's narrative heart.

Sweet times, we fantasized
you were our secret child, hermaphrodite
hidden beneath the gentle floor,
and I imagined slipping you gifts
through furnace ducts—cookies
or a blanket, a silver flute,
baritone arms to comfort your solo soprano.

You never mentioned insults annealed
as wind storming the air vents nor doors
that slammed above your head, but
when my love revved out the drive,
you sang Violetta as you brewed for me
chamomile tea in your favorite lilac cup.

Friends joked about my affection
but I recalled the girl who loved Quasimodo,
another who rode the white bear's back
beyond the sun and moon. I did not care
how completely your boy face aged in sun,
revealing a grandmother's veins beating blue.

After your smash debut in Figaro, you
told me you were moving to L.A.,
and I worried about the lack of shade,
the race of giants who live for sun.
Who would love your face?

Spirit beneath the deadly clamor of our lives singing,
I didn't believe I'd survive without your melodies
steaming up like healing vapors.

White bear, didn't Athena after long wars
discover her own delicate hands?
Even vain Cupid learned to reconcile love's discords
shaped like you, soft as a woman.

Now, a decade gone, my love and I embrace
surviving desert heat and tropic gusts
that threaten fragile lemon blooms in our tranquil yard.
Sometimes I listen to the longing arpeggio of doves
and hear sweet octaves scale
your throat, dwarfing all sorrow.

Tonight beneathe the endless crescendo of stars, I look to
black iridescent night, to those rare Blue Dwarfs
who flare the hottest bloom.

THE MINOTAUR

after an etching by James G. Davis

Suppose he's not given to revenge,
                       Still, he must
     dream of Ariadne
and feel a little sad
when he thinks of the waxed thread ball.
Perhaps she'd tried the trick first, and
         he remembers the taste of cloves on her breath,
            why he'd slept
so long the next day.

Suppose he's not given to revenge.
         Still, fists are startling alarm clocks
and he cannot forget dying.
           Perhaps, even now, when he drinks
too much,
     he smells nettles,
then his blood spicing Theseus's hands.

       Sometimes, the minotaur remembers
too much, exiled with his own walls
sunk under roots.
He is a little like us,
     perhaps wears jeans,
hides in his cave and, when night
comes on, he hears
his own shadow coming home.

If we visited him,
>   we'd wonder
at the skull sprouting child's arms
like a philodendron under the TV,
>   the dog-faced roast
untouched on his table,
>   but he'd tell us
after all these years
he's learned about metaphor
and he'd smile that crooked bull's smile,
his horns white as skate blades
>   shaking his dark arena.

He is alone most nights
and often fingers with man's fingers
his ragged beast's head.

He owns no mirrors
>   but knows each shifting image
between cloven hoof
and human ankle, between
>   thin voice and shaggy face.

He's not given to revenge

but some nights the road
brings a car, maybe
carrying a family home from a picnic.
Not revenge
>   but his shadow leaps
out before him onto the dusky lane
and the car skids in nettles.

Maybe the family won't talk
about the monster they've seen,
saying it was something silly like
a trick of the eye.

It is then, dreaming of Ariadne's face,
round as a waxed thread ball,
the Minotaur waves, calling back
the white faces like balloons startled
in the windows rushing by.

WATERCOLORIST IN THE STREAM

for Bruce McGrew

The shattered piping of canyon wrens
flutes across sandstone cliffs
while you shoulder the drawing board
like some stiff-winged angel
and wade into Aravaipa Creek.

This stream's magic is to vanish
beneath its own bed a mile east.
Here mud sculpins, dragonfish
and rare darters start like dark flames
from your toes edging upstream.

Your eyes assess perspective and shadows
on uprooted cottonwoods, wrecked javelina bones
and cactus cast by a flashflood
that rearranged the valley.

To spot rare species of birds, we climb
while you discover
                the place you'll render,
a gorgeous luminaria of river shade.

Taking the wide bend, you
soak rag paper and begin,
lift brushes to test the wind, alert
above light's blank raw fields.

The first stroke is crucial as the flexing wing
is to the final music of any bird—
each resolution of color to nerve,
      eye-song to heart,
invents form from the oomphalos of time.

Each pigment devises its own vision
of the canyon's sheer rock shoulders, interprets
heat bursting the mineral light of water
that eddies behind your knees.

You paint what your eyes dream.
Cobalt blue and aquamarine
fuse the ripe spines of jumping cholla,
      prickly pear and creosote bush.
Your hand flies, and granite splits
in a flash of titanium
white as the glass talons of wind.

Intuitive mediums, your fingers brush
a single slash of cadmium yellow
that defines
         the exact center of a sulfur moth's flight.
From your heart's landscape
you translate earth into a liquid language
old as human need.

Sky opens your skin, and you believe
ancestors never die,
love will not betray you,
and each severed tongue of hope is resewn
whole and fully articulate

as color conjuring the blind page.

It is left for us who search out wild birds,
the solitude of constant sun and endangered breeds,
to come upon you ordering chaos
where we first learned to breathe.

Water is your metaphor
refracting a thousand fingernails of light.
Heading back downstream, we leave you
to the wide loops of a redtail hawk
whose hunting scream circles everything
we imagine we understand.
Into desert's vast horizon
            the current disappears.
We are consumed by such astounding shadows.

DOMESTIC PASSION

    for Bill

All fall they've stopped us.
Wheeling above Tucson or that afternoon
        skinning the dry San Jacinto river
etched against cliffs the color of doeskin,
          Redtailed Hawks sliced sunset, talons
knifing each other's spiral dive, screeching fights
we finally recognized as mating cries.
That fierce domestic passion
    silenced every one of us
as they tore the tranquil silk of sky's blue throat.

With your daughter, hiking a Pasadena creek
while traffic raked its nails across brittle hills,
we watched the heart-dropped swoop of two hawks
like a couple long married,
loving despite tainted updrafts
they rode, bloodcopper tails
        fanning afternoon wild
as they slashed one another's flight, coupling.

You show me the Harris Hawks,
elegant pair feathered in formal attire,
that terrorized our backyard while I was teaching.
Atop the electric pole, they took turns
ripping red chunks of pigeon
from thin bones,

screaming like wrenched sheets of steel,
    as if the city didn't exist, as if
their gore-stained beaks
and frozen lemon eyes were their own domicile.

Love, how I admire
these winter hawks, surviving
    in desert air we breathe to sustain us.

BATHING IN

KACHINA HOT SPRINGS

Is this scorching a lightning bolt's remnants,
or the burning mountain?
The heat of my sighs, or your inner body?

– Bibi Hayati, Sufi Poet

BATHING AT KACHINA HOT SPRINGS

for Teresa Acevedo

I

We unmoor from our bodies,
anemones healing in the thermal stream,
faces tilted like sunflowers
toward sun's bloody hieroglyph
inscribed behind our closed lids.

Each muscle seized is undone
at the sacred feet of Mt. Graham
where Geronimo spins, come back as a dust devil,
his broad shoulders a dervish of gold sand.
He dances down deer to browse.
From their mouths, time breathes.

Otter woman, water bearer, you bask in healing steam,
dream clay half-fills your ancestral home
in Aravaipa Canyon, where
your grandfathers farmed deltas
and the dark slopes of night,
where moon-eyed as coyotes
they hunted jack rabbits, deer
and big-horn sheep along
the limber song of the creek they adored.
At the millennium's breach, your family
can't recall their Opata tongues.

You dream your canyon crumbles
like dry tortillas, half-fills with clay
and you lie mummified,
relic of love and questions
returned to the hands of sandstone
and wind who spun your shape
while I converse with deer who gather
in a high meadow, circling.

> *Sing, your charge is to sing. Get the story right.*
> *Heat flattens us, then apocalyptic storms save everything.*
> *Ocean becomes desert and earth becomes the wind.*
> *Even earth can tire of spring.*

II

Think of Geronimo, how, deciphering each
direction of wind, he defied decades of soldiers,
                              how today he turned up
like a dinner invitation from a lost friend,
knocking on the red door of our rental car,
then led us to these pools to dream
after we drove your disabled mother
to her trailer in Safford, fed her tortillas,
chicken and the seven steroids
the doctor prescribed for crippling arthritis,
your mother who all of her life cleaned
the houses of the rich and infirm.

My mother, whose body bends like a questioning reed,
tends my invalid father she's loved
half a century, and now she goes blind.
Nurses binding the world's wounds,
where is justice and
what is our true legacy?

Drifting in sulfur steam, my body
half-keels, rights itself, a lost raft,
bouy of time and fortune,
and I look up in time for a redtailed hawk
to split the sky we breathe,
cleaving the deer's green song,
my heart's four-chambered melody
naked in my naked chest, a hawk
who clutches its own death shriek
in its killing beak.

How many ways there are
                    to die, then
the upswing to survive.

Women precipiced at midlife, we wonder
which choices bring down the stars,
which turn to lead slugs that clog the machine.

Childless women, we are armed against loneliness
with the certainty of the deer's obsidian climb
up hardscrabble cliffs, scored
by the hawk's quick scree.

Childless women, our shadows must create
             love, then

          my friend, we come home,
          home to liquid arms sweetening the center
          of rock old as need, home.
          We have arrived.

III

You and I are bright as mica afloat
in memory's long aquamarine pool,
our thighs brushing, breasts
and stomachs refashioned
by the mineral hands of water
from the mountain that interprets sky.
We fall into constellations our grandmothers
named for our sakes.

          Blue mountain, sacred
          mountain, bloodied
          by dawn, by dusk's stigmata,
          peaks astonished by a flurry of wings
          outlasting all questioning.
          Holy mountain bulldozed
          for government contracts,
          for the telescope extending astronomer's eyes.

Do you hear your grandmother
calm as Aravaipa cliffs, see her

unlined hands squeeze clay
to shape pots into the heads of deer,
the sweet piping of canyon wrens.
What lightning haloes her head,
divides the rocks?

My grandmother warns me
as she weaves a mat of strawberry grass
and dandelion greens. *Love,*
love hard, love
wide as the sunbent heart of wind
that defines everything.
> *Keep your eye to the horizon*
> *beyond betrayal,*
> *beyond destruction, beyond greed,*
> my grandmother sings,
velvet moth relieved of her husbands' deceits,
velvet moth green and intelligent as the moon.

I turn my face in the water
and your dark hair angels your profile
carved from the mask of Mayan Jaguar Kings.
I remember how the pyramids terrified your soul,
how in a rainforest where the quetzel flies,
you found your own obsidian head
buried deep in earth.

Oh, sweet sister, to sweat like this
in the torrid afternoon sheets of late summer,
neck deep in a thermal sea
miraculous in a desert thirsty as its name.

Oh, to leak all sorrow,
all grief of the might have been
children, the rainless seasons dictating our wombs.

We sleep in the numinous hands of water
piped from the lucid hearts
of granite cliffs duplicating themselves
like giant star clusters, laughing
in their shifting coats of blue mist
above the spin of Geronimo,
above the porcelain clatter of deer hooves
      tapping out the syllabics of desire
between arid thorns,
      above the hawk digesting her kill,
          above the near coil of the rattler
loving us, loving us.

IV

Now it is migration time,
the thick afternoon before the harvest moon.
Outside the cotton is waist deep,
slick green leaves,
hives of pesticides
insulting the ancient peaks.
Is it any wonder Geronimo drills anger to the four winds,
that hawk bones thin, eggshells
crack, arthritis cribs joints
shattering of their own weight.

Who can breathe tonight?

Your mother says so many people
get cancer here in this valley,
even couples die sixty days apart.
The spray is like gauze in her face.
Cotton growers complain they're going broke
but who holds all those coins?

V

I touch your hand
soft as velvet dust on a moth's wing
that glides each lick of tide
moving the shore of this old sea we navigate.

Dear friend, when you die
into another life, who will kiss
your wrists alive?
We enter the sacred waters,
the water enters us
until we evaporate into wind
that scales the clarified octaves above treeline,
witnessing everything,
unmoved, undestroyed symphony
radiant with gravity, with passing light.

VI

Geronimo bends to stroke away the lines
dividing our sight, stills lightning
that would slice dreams from our long journey.

He is our witness
as much as that hawk,
cocking his vain head,
his yellow eye entering ours
above the eternal pitch of his cry—
          the mnemonic shapes, hunter and prey
and the lines that blur,
changing everything.

What can we know
except those we love
and the stories brambling our lives?

In the arroyo throb
strobed between my eyes, we dance
spinning naked as lotuses, our tongues
untied as our grandmothers'
ululating the clear syntax of stars,
metaphors of hope and wind
against sorrow, against greed.

You lie still as an altar
in blue water, your skin's brown clay
kneaded by your grandmother's fingers,
while your mother's arthritic clasp
is restored sweet and lithe
as the first music
calling the cells of the hawk to fly.

CALENDAR OF THIRST

Speak to the stones, and the stars answer.
At first the visible obscures:
Go where light is.

– Theodore Roethke

IT IS PRECISELY

that I can bite
into the crisp red hide of an apple
without the shadow of a bar
dissecting my throat as it swallows
that river of unlegislated juice

that I can slide into a pair of worn jeans
to dig crab grass from purple verbenas
I planted last spring without the crimp
of a fist bursting my kidney under a thin shirt
prolaiming the freedom of its ragged borders

that I can whirl words in the clear tumbler
of any poem I wake at any hour to brew
without the manacles of fear
clamping my wrists behind my back
turned on the interrogator's slit lips.

that I can watch the thousand bullets
burn mouths into the singing backs of girls
and boys crushed with their questions
by the tanks and bombs of the world
without prison walls blinding my heart
that witnesses the long sting of history

I cannot close my eyes

LATE ELEGY

*for Alaide Foppa, kidnapped
by the Guatelmalan Army in 1980*

Slick as volcanic clay, fevered as the assassination of stars,
a poem is born from the bones of a woman
who cultivated the million patiences
it took to raise five children
along with four forbidden books.

Who can answer for the ski-masked soldiers
who snatched this mother
from the exact intersection of her children
with ink illuminating her soul
in the vein-blue stanza of a Guatemalan night
so that her lips never again shaped
the syllabics of truth on earth?

And who can positively spin
the tale of jungle flies
feasting on the corpse of the mother
        who wrote, "I hear poetry
like a secret disease, a hidden illicit fruit"
        so that she would be forgotten
as soon as the murdered audience?

A poem was born this afternoon, slick
as wet clay streaking a mountain road
a column of soldiers skids across

as they patrol, triggering
random slugs into Indians and torching the rainforest,
a poem blue as the Guatemalan air
a helicopter chops into verse
before it is snuffed like a cigarette or a jaw under a boot.

CALENDAR OF THIRST

for Lyndy Cranson and Leslie Marmon Silko

I

It's the rainy season and it's raining dust.
Across the valley, dust devils sway like drunks.
Fahrenheit breaks a hundred and ten. Tucson sweats.
Summer and the old Sonoran soft shoe.

II

I water the thirsty—the Russian olive
with its armloads of silver marquis leaves,
three thorny orange trees,
the soberly elegant Italian cypresses,
penstimon, oleanders and geraniums
knotted as arthritics
fingering the broken keyboard of the fence.
I make a moat around the fig
bent with soft green fruit.
Rain's weeks overdue
and there isn't enough water to hold
down grit that grooms the yard
with hot smoke brushes.

III

On Main, men squat in the adobe shade
of walls renovated by lawyers
who sit fixed by appointments.
Who's suing who?
Transients from everywhere drink
wine and quarts of beer from paper bags,
their faces stained dark as hauraches.
Time is a narcotic argument pushed by constant sun.
Our almanac predicted a dry year.
Cicadas concur, whirring in Palo Verde or fir,
their a cappella a perfect democracy
above drunk and financier,
above the lawyer and civil disputes
or his secretary in her white heels
spiking against the light to save time.

IV

West, in this same desert,
eighteen illegal aliens are found sealed
in a boxcar, dead from thirst.
Daily, others lose their way
across mica and broken granite
all along the border, until
they enter a final dry valley
where, out of water and luck, they
drink aftershave, suck toothpaste tubes flat.

Then mirages overtake them,
and they forget betrayal, life savings
spent on promises of employment north.
Nothing, no railroad official,
no Coyote bribed, can refund the lives
of these men and women beyond any law, now,
their tongues swollen black.

V

The yard dizzies in heat. Everything tipples
but the lizard keeping to the shade of the olive
as he dances down scaly bark
to the flood pooling from my garden hose
where bugs swim circles,
unconcerned about the water's source.

VI

Consider the Mayan calendar
which, like the nautilus reaching
its iridescent center, ends this year, mid-August.
What is the apocalypse
to the lawyer with his golden tan
or to the drunks leaning into clay walls
that soften with each pass of the bottle?
To the vulture the ultimate harmony
is his convergence with the corpse.
The Day of the Dead is celebrated
graveside with fiesta and food.

VII

The lizard measures each second he hunts,
his reflection broken by insects
spinning across the glass bulge of the pool.
In one lance thrust, his tongue catches
what the ground's given up,
a segmented beetle with a forked pincer tail.

The lizard doesn't consider its ugliness
as he twirls the beetle like a baton,
gulps it down, whole, a lump lost
to the stomach's tympanum
stretched pink under arid skin.

VIII

Sky holds the blue spear of its season
against clouds that would form like cauliflower fists
to beat dust from the Catalinas,
the Rincons, the Tucson Mountains.
Time in a bottle.
Sky waits.

IX

I remember the delirious summer a woman
staggered up and down Main.
Wrapped in black plastic under mumbling noon sun,
I couldn't miss her.

Even drunks shunned her.
At night she was the Siren
who screamed outside my sister's house
until the police came.
She couldn't generate enough heat
to incinerate the insects of suffering
that drank her heart.
Each time she was sent to the psychiatric ward
doctors released her to poverty,
sweat, garbage bags that tore
like old veils around her red ankles.
She carried no bottles or drugs, so far
beyond those devils that melt time, was she.
In vacant lots she drew sundials,
damning all of us.

X

Now I water the trees and wonder
about the calendar and its circular walls.
How does the nautilus end?
Hot wind blasts the valley
while dust devils my yard.
Even lizard closes his eyes
against this long season, debris
flung like shrapnel
as he hunts the miraculous pool
and its shipload of foolish bugs.

RATTLER

And the slumber of the body seems to be
but the waking of the soul.
        – Sir Thomas Browne

Soundless as sun lodging in glass,
rock sweats under me
sleeping naked at the dry waterfall.
Desert birds find shade,
and I am fever slipping into stone.
Lost to heat, arms
and legs dissolve midair.
Obedient to gravity, I slide
against granite, displacing my skin
with scales that bite like metal.

In my dream, I find water and swim
through rainlit reeds near shore
startled by your warm almond scent.
Snake, you slip so silent
your smooth skin doesn't disturb me
dreaming you.
I wake when your tail clatters
like marbles spilt on a slate floor.
On the rock shelf above my head
you coil six feet of muscle.

Your eyes never shut.
With your severed tongue
you've always hunted fear.

Now you offer no apple
just your rattle fluent
as a lover's sudden goodbye.
The pure syntax of light,
you are flat as gold, flickering
as the silver afterthought of winter.

    You don't strike
when I jump to another rock
split in a margin of shade.
            You rise while I rise
in the yellow brain of your reptilian eyes.
Our heads weave agreement
as we stare, caught
by the communication we remember from sleep,
our truce old.

WITHOUT THE COMFORT OF STARS

I

Through leaky blinds a tropical moon prepares
its own execution:
the jaguar who'll swallow whole light
and the bloody sins of the world.

Without the comfort of stars, moon swings up,
a cat skull bedraggled and glaring
at temperamental thunderheads that javelined
salt cedar limbs into tiled roofs.

Who knows why it rains through
the driest season of the desert's heart.
Meteorologists calculate the jet stream's coquetry,
track El Niño's adolescent fevers.
Our yard's lost to muddy surf
I broom back from the door.
The city reeks of crushed gardenias,
wet dog shit, delicious creosote.

II

Each sound outgrows its skin:
slosh of tires negotiating torrents, police
sirens and car alarms that melt trees.

Somewhere between this desert turned
Mississippi delta and New York,
the man I love flies into the same storms
that stripped all our roses.

I light a candle and pray him home
then flick on late news in time to see
Israeli soldiers fire point blank into Palestinians
shopping on their own West Bank.

High caliber bullets slam near
an old woman carrying a cardboard box
atop her head. Like a black leaf
blown against quivering adobe,
she looks like anyone's grandmother
about to be gunned down.

III

What hands will sew wings
for her, bulletproof wings
to whisk her beyond blood tithe, the tantrum
of automatic revenge? And if she survives
unscathed, who will brew honey tea,
wring out a cool cloth
to soothe her throbbing temple,
rub rosemary oil into her thin wrists?
The camera's eye loses the woman,
and I pretend she lives,
she lives.

Through the window the moon's pared
slick as an icy fang, and I recall
that Mayan priests interpreted the eclipse
as a jaguar who ate the bloody moon
to spare the people harm.

IV

Jaguar, tonight chew the moon.
While rain scours desert clean, teach us
greening songs. Bring old women wings.

SIMON'S STORY

Over noon sandwiches and gossip about
class discipline, the Nigerian student teacher tells
that his friend, a journalist, blew open
the military regime's addiction to torture, to erasing
citizens like graffiti defiling Lagos streets.
From midnight dreams, the writer, his wife, daughter
and infant son were dragged to the police van.
To add to the rubberhose strope of beatings,
guards flooded prison cells, knee-deep.

So the baby wouldn't drown in his sleep,
father and mother took turns rocking him
in the cradle of their outstretched arms.
The metal cuffs bit through their wrists.

For weeks, the family turned amphibian,
eating meals in water,
shitting in water, sleeping in water,
in shifts by squatting with their heads
propped against the slimy wall.
They never saw their swollen feet.

Loud speakers infected sunrises and sunsets
they never saw behind stone walls
while humid mosquitoes drilled each open sore
so that mother and father slurred
simple consonants of reassurance

they would have fed their children.
In that congested lung of interrogation,
to stay alive, they bartered screams
for lullabies.

How can I ever answer Simon's far eyes
dismantling the elementary school walls.
What luxury it is to write in this country, knowing
I am spoiled, insisting on truth
that has so little consequence.
Visa nearly expired, Simon smiles,
"They were the lucky ones." His tattooed cheeks
    rise round and kind as blue gourds.
      "My friends escaped."

NEW SCIENCE

In the unmade light I can see the world.
       – W.S. Merwin

Morning and everything is unmade in the sky—
the kingbird diving for gnats that cloud to mine blood
the gnats black as the weevil at the heart of desire
desire the heart of the sulfur wings of kingbirds
and everything unmade and unsaleable

In this desert there is no gene splicing
no recombinant DNA or genetic engineering of species
no mixing of pig and horse, human and cow to invent
the perfect breed, no test-tube tomatoes
with doubled shelf lives, no growth hormones
to reverse aging in 70 year old men, just morning
and the kingbird's unmade light, ascending

TO MAKE THE BULL ASCEND

for Joy Fox McGrew

The clay must suggest air,
forelegs spread to wings, glaze
stroked white on pale iron oxide.
Slick as a wet luna moth set for flight,
vertebrae align beneath the pelvic girdle
that flares into a crude heart.
Where the real heart would lie
two bisque petals burst unfolding wings.

Everything is suspended under the bull's head,
his horn forever curled
to the broken tip with its hint of brutality.
Tilted up, the bovine face is
all contrast, gunmetal
matte enlightened with glyphs—
                a saguaro cactus, one
blinking Valentine, inverted
knock-kneed goats.
The eye is feminine, Egyptian
and slender, gazing above the masculine
cheekbone, the mouth's quizzical slit.

To make the bull ascend
the whole body must be cocked starward,
male and female balanced, carefully masquerading
as a sculpture nailed to the wall.

CARETAKING

The young cat, manic, spins
      to swat at caustic ants
that crawl up from the cracks in the floor.
She has learned the bitterness of tannic acid
and no longer bites them. They say
El Niño breeds termites and mosquitos,
but these ants march everywhere
sidestepping each guaranteed trap, raiding
kitchen cabinets, queuing up
like columns of colons punctuating doors.

This dawn, before the Mockingbird rang up desert sun
my head cocked like a trigger on the pillow,
      my hands fisted the quilt. Over and over
I blew smil to the four frantic directions
while my dream mother, blind and psychotic,
crouched like a young ratmole behind me.
She refused to protect herself, so
I swatted at her terrors, squared my hips
      between her and whatever I could never see.

I wake to the telephone's staccato ring,
my mother's wrenched soprano demanding to know
why chainsaws are chopping the fingers
from her invisible son's hands. I remind her
that she is blind, her son thousands of miles away.
"Rest," I say, "go back to sleep"

as I watch the cat, outnumbered by ants.
Giving up, she oozes back to my safe bed,
purring even as she claws my arm.
The cat can never win against the fecundity of insects
nor discover
      from which cracks they will rise next.

THROUGH THE DARK, A BRILLIANCE

for Judi and Val

You always think the untended will fail
        like the amaryllis
left for months in a dark bedroom.
And it is deserved
if its leaves turn brown and it slumps
around its pot, not like the rose
you dutifully prune,
pinching off dead blossoms
to make way for the new.
The rose you believe is immortal,
a Lazarus you guard so close
the petals blind you to the roots, the way
they rot in floods underground.
When it finally dies, despite
fertilizers, the patient attention
to blooms, you wonder
why it reminds you of love
whose showiness promises
the illusion you sustain,
not wanting to know what navigates there
like blind fish in subterranean streams.

Then, you remember the amaryllis,
        its own shepherdess,
who even now sprouts the stalk
whose bud will become

the trumpeting blossom, a brilliance
that is a surprise sustaining itself
through months of dark and mysterious longings
your careful hands would learn.

Then I came street by street, river by river,
city by city, bed by bed,
and my brackish masquerade crossed the desert,
until in the last humble houses, without lamps, without fire,
without bread, without stone, without silence, alone,
I paced, dying of my proper death.

– Pablo Neruda

PAROLE

an elegy for Andres Herendez, alias Picasso

I

The wall I face is nailed with skulls
deer
javelinas
the delicate bleached bones of raccoons.
Picasso, you would have liked it
in this desert studio
far from the diseases of the humid east.
I'm surrounded by myth
formed in clay, glazes
dug from poorest earth,
sculptures like the dream of life
on every wall, knocked awake.
And paintings, thick oils
your heart's tongue would have licked
like cream.
Had you not been born poor
in Puerto Rico,
had you not gone to prison at sixteen,
dropout killer,
armed robber.
Had your father not abandoned
your asthmatic mother before you could walk, could fly
from the everyday heat
of tin-shacked streets, raw sewage

that fed ragged palms outside your door.
What a rich Siren
New York must have seemed.

II

I bring you here, now, thousands of miles
from your common grave marked only by a number.
Convict, your name can never be added
to the quilt, though you died
no less than your brothers from AIDS
alone in the secret hospital, died
choking on your own blood,
with no immunity left for this world.

Is your mind still a seabird, Andres,
circling the thousand verses you memorized
to lighten your sentence, singing
defiant above the wrecked shore of your body?

III

Your final gift to me was
the book of poems you loved —
Neruda, Lorca, Paz, Rudolfo —
the only law you imagined
fired you beyond the steel bite of bars,
poems bound in red leather,
with gold leaf letters —
eleganté — poems

from your own singing tongue.
I don't care if the book was stolen
it burns
like the skin of angels in my hands.

What mourning gift can I make for your memory
but this poem born in a desert
purified by the innocent hands of wind
that live by their own laws?
My student, the last day
you came to class, you insisted
I take this book.

I hardly knew you and wanted to escape
the torn olive curtains
and volatile perfume of cooped-up men
crushing cigarette after cigarette into the floor.

Hunched over, you couldn't stop coughing
        but your eyes were gray lasers that held
back the guard who ordered you out.

You stood and recited,

> *entonces fui por calle y calle y rio y rio*
> *y cuidad y cuidad y cama y cama*
> *y atravesó el desierto mi mascara salobre,*
> *y en las ultimas casas humilladas, sin lampara, sin fuego,*
> *sin pan, sin piedra, sin silencio, solo,*
> *rodé muriendo de mi propia muerte.*

IV

Other inmates called you Picasso,
old man who could sketch anything,
who recited poems as he brushed
his vision of the perfect universe
in mural mountains and eagles,
the wide ungovernable sea, to
transform the shame of thick cement walls
warehousing the disinherited.

Andres, we never find anything too late.
Nor anyone.
As you lay dying, the warden denied
my every request,
denied all visitors
but the distant rags of your family
too destitute to make such a trip,
denied even get well cards.
After all, you were maximum security.
But nothing can bar this final poem,
this farewell kiss from a stranger
who was the teacher you taught.

LATE WINTER STORM

in memory of Victor Jara

No one bets on the cockfight
of wind and snow.
No one antes; no one could win.
A thousand beaks of ice bite
when spring should start.
Confined, we turn
to the tape of your singing,
your voice an angelic blade
that skins the whole house.
Outside, the cockfight claws
above the mourning dove
who navigates drifts, scratching
for seeds beneath the lilac
and its blasted blooms.

Your voice dreams equality,
honey dabbed across poverty's wounds,
love's citrus flowers set
like topaz suns in blue rain,
and Chile, liberated as the sea.
Your voice dreams.
Los manos negros.
Los manos blancos.
Son los mismos, Victor.

Children should eat but
the hands of generals seldom turn furrows,
and fields become graves.
Peruvian pipes flute sweet knives of longing.
The house is not large enough
for the memory of the day
you were led by the comandante
into the stadium, where the arrested
six thousand were forced to watch
as he ordered you to spread your hands
on the table placed dead center in the arena,
forced to watch
as the comandante lifted his machete,
to watch
as he chopped your fingers from each hand,
to watch
the comandante curse then beat you
with his whole fists, beat you
while your startled hands bled to dust.

This house can never be large enough.
Victor, today you live in each room,
holding up your arms
like bouquets of dripping roses
in front of us.
Your songs held so many hands,
hands of honey,
los manos de sangre,
los manos perdidos,
son los mismos.
How do our hearts survive?

See the seven angels of hope
charge each other with golden swords?
Who can remove the generals now
Allende's dead, Neruda's dead,
and so many disappeared from the streets,
and you,
oh, Victor, and you?
No one charged from his seat
in that stadium to stop the blood
or the comandante
even when he demanded, "Sing, now,
you bastard. Sing!"

So you sang.
Offering your arms to the crowd, you sang.
And they answered,
singing louder and louder, the anthem
of the Unidad Popular.
Until the machine guns burst you,
until the machine guns burst the crowd.
How could the soldiers' hearts survive?

Even now they cannot stop
the doves lifting from your guitar strings
into these rooms so far North.

They cannot stop your voice
men could live or die for.

Wind bites away the world
and we recall what politics demand we forget,
what the sea can never wash from land.

It never ends.
All across the globe's wobbling spin, generals
topple one another like drunks.
Their cockfights never end.
The people still starve.

Victor, wake us now
with your hands and the red wine
of their truth, wake us
in this stunted season,
wake us with your songs.
Bring back the oranges,
the lilacs waiting for new blooms!

WALKING ON THE OTHER SIDE OF TWILIGHT

with LuLu in an old Tucson neighborhood
where colonial Spanish grilled adobe casas
with iron bars to keep out the natives,
we breathe as much dust as air.

Desert earth yearns for clouds,
for rain to love it clean.
All the spring poppies have dropped
their crepe petals and thorns
thicken the smallest branches of mesquite.

Each day I teach poetry in Barrio Libre,
the way truth and illusion create images,
to the great grandchildren of Cortez
and Zapata, William Bonnie and Cochise.
Still at war they cruise by in booming lowriders
or jacked-up pickups slick as wet jaguars.
Gunshots rock their dreams
in semi-automatic inquisitions of revenge.
They would shoot their own grandfathers
for flashing the wrong sign. What
sign can I give them?

Cool, Miss, drive-bys are cool, suavecito.
I remember the third grader, smile
jittery as amphetamines, when he described in one breath,
his uncle shot in the back and the new batch of puppies
born in his bedroom the night before.

WAITING FOR RAIN

There are three things that will not be satisfied,
Four that will never cry, "Enough!" –
Sheol, a barren womb, a land short of water,
And fire which never cries "Enough!"

Proverbs 30: 15b-16

WAITING FOR RAIN

for Bill and Jennifer

I

Tiny lines track the corners of my eyes,
crowfoot testament to sleepless quarrels,
all worries, petty or not.
I wake in glass, my face cloned
and distant there.
I wake in glass
watching an Orb Weaver spin silk webs
while children wrestle over her back.

In the mirror, I stretch my neck
with a monster smile, lifting my breasts.
Firm as nectarines, they
dare gravity, wonder what mystery
a small mouth might urge.

I'm thirty-three,
born the third Zodiac sign, oldest
of three sisters and their luck.
I pray for monsoons,
lightning to snap my ground.
My third marriage rummages up from dreams
as I rinse my face, convinced
this obsession with threes must end

or another year will pass,
dangerous as any lover who called me beautiful
too often to believe.

II

Thunder lifts the dry turrets of mountains
while the first electric air before a storm
dyes desert improbably green.

                    We admire the wide mind of sky
whose seasons shift each hour,
whose light is the face of memory
old as carbon, young as wind.

Rising at sunset, the Sacred Datura
blossoms white one night,
dies with stars, its whole sexuality
complete before the moon sets.
                    And after each day's rain,
bent to our front door,
new blooms!

What passes between lovers
in houses held tight against storms,
we only guess as we reinvent
each new and familiar touch.

Love, your eyes follow flashes
that split the clouds' dark breasts.

You bite my lips and rise
while lightning dies
of its own crazy bursts.

III

ein Drang nach dem kinde
My dog is pregnant and lies
in the shade. Her eight breasts stretch
charmed as Kali's
whose witched milk fed all.
Her eyes are narrow black moons.
She speaks
in low moan, is virgin,
one-in-herself.
                Ishtar
Artemis
Aphrodite soon forgot their mates.
My dog is pregnant.
I love her slow bloom as each day
she opens, grows radiant
as air after typhoons.

If I had a daughter, I'd hold
her fingers to this dog
and gentle them across
thick wrigglings under fur,
telling her that this is only one thing
vessels are used for.

My stomach is flat.
I don't know what to do.
What to do. Remember
      how quick rain boils
down dry riverbeds,
      wetting topsoil enough
to make grasses grow, enough to polish
manzanitas blood-bright.

IV

Love, you leave with your daughter
to wander Grand Canyon and marvel
at all the colors harvested by sky.
Each vista will multiply
until your minds refuse the infinite
they can't take in.
When you hike back to your small camp,
light and shadows will scour
your faces like angels.
There will be storms tonight.
What will you tell her?

One night, driving with my father, I saw
a tree on fire in the middle of a field.
It rouged the faces of Hereford cattle
lowing around it, a bodiless chorus
above white and cloven hooves.
At home, my mother, mad with ghosts,
prophecized the tree meant
someone else we loved would die.

For months, my mother was gone,
drugged in soft rooms.
Visiting her we passed an old woman
cradling an empty blanket who sang
      lost, lost, lost
to its blue folds.

I remember my mother's screams
for her children to save her,
but I was too young and ran out,
sick all the way home.

Mother, I am still saving you.
In some sterile room within my heart,
a stone swells, fixing its curse
on seed that would germinate there.
If we could only find the clue,
we could split it with an ax
honed blue as thunder.

V

Walking in the last pools of sunlight
along the wash, I kneel
to gather the scattered feathers of the Phainopepla
killed last night.
Its black and white flight primaries
cross its drying bones.
Already ants swarm in silt,
salting its body.

Tomorrow it will be consumed,
only these feathers saved.
I wait for rain.
          There is no wind,
just the distant tympanum
and the small clatter of birds finding a roost.
Child, would you disturb
this quiet that bathes me like myrrh?
Or, in sharing your endless questions, would I
find rest for mine?

For years I've owned silence,
cultivating it, knowing
seeds thrived or died at whim.
Each intruder I murdered with resentment.

You, who fail to grow within me,
frighten my dreams
with your small red hands.

          Child, I give you this solitude,
storms teasing the horizon's wide mouth.

Teach me the waters
that hide you.

VI

Our first dreams levitate
inside the dividing cell, swim careless
as phosphorescent fish

seeing all but themselves.
Later we wake or fly
in those falling nightmares
whose black landings could kill us.

We climb to cliff's edge
disintegrating with each step, and before
we jump, we remember
dropping from our mothers,
our mutual understanding broken.

In other dreams, we search for openings
through which we might fly
from horses who rear
behind the moon's boney eye.
Their hooves are anthracite,
their wombs dilate red mouths
calling us where the dead gather
among fires white as silk.

Child, there is never enough time.
In this land of thirsty arroyos
dreams are as quick to disappear
as lizards running for shade.

VII

Love, tomorrow you come back.
                    Testing each curve
that gives or firms, I perfume
                    my skin with hibiscus,

wash my hair in lemon, brush it
                 shining around my breasts.

Tonight there will be a new moon, its thin arms
above us,
discovering their exact capacity.

Quiet as dusk, the Datura dies
into its seductive blooms.
Moon-blessed and lovely, even closed,
it draws water up through its poisonous roots,
sister to Belladonna,
Deadly Nightshade.
A pinch of its pollen brings strange dreams.

A wind snakes in from the South,
cool as scales, and stars
extinguish, devoured by voluptuous clouds.
On the dark porch, leaf-bright
mantises stalk their mates.
From lightning veins, ozone
splashes, musk-ripe,
as I walk out in this thirty-third year
to meet the slashing rain
that could open my house.